Brother C

Continue to ..... and know that God is in charge. Keep the faith.

The Alphabet of Self-Esteem:

An Inspirational Journal for Successful Living

Lawrence J. Hanks, Ph.D.

Lawrence J. Hanks

04 / 17 / 04

© 2004 by Lawrence J. Hanks. All rights reserved.

No part of this book may be reproduced, stored in a retrieval system, or transmitted by any means, electronic, mechanical, photocopying, recording, or otherwise, without written permission from the author.

ISBN: 1-4140-4038-5 (e-book)
ISBN: 1-4140-4037-7 (Paperback)
ISBN: 1-4140-4036-9 (Hardcover)

This book is printed on acid free paper.

1st Books - rev. 1/20/04

Dedication

For Shonda Latrice,
my first child

You were a wonderful and flawless child,
You are a wonderful and flawless adult

Carpe Diem
Know that you are loved !

ACKNOWLEDGEMENTS

While one individual may conceptualize an idea, actualization of the idea usually requires a collective effort. This book would not be possible without the support of a plethora of people. I am thankful and grateful to God for showing up in the following people:

My wife, Diane Gordon Hanks, for her unwavering support
My mother, Kathleen Williams Hanks, for her unconditional love
My progeny, Shonda Latrice, L. Julius, II, Latoysha Joy, and Mahogany Arlette

My siblings and their spouses, Edmond and Frances Hanks Cook, Carolyn Hanks Holley, Hasan Hanks and Julie Barbot, and W. Paul Hanks

My aunts, Mamie Williams Bryant, Marie Stephens, and Susan Williams

My publicist, Estella Kirk Stovall

Very special friends: Rick Morgenstern, Michael Gordon, T. Michael Ford, James Mumford, Adlai Pappy, Adverse Ponder, Oliver Hunter, Livia Sapp, Horace Allen, Oliver Robinson, Vincent Stovall, Edward Wheeler, Louis Stovall, and Cheryl Jones Pappy

My Morehouse Brothers and their families: Oliver, Sharon, Adam, and Noah Robinson; Adlai, Cheryl, Adlai II (my god-son), and Camille Pappy; Vincent, Lorraine, and Somerlyn Stovall; Elton, Laura, Sya, Evan, and Christina Gaddy; Adverse and Iyanth Ponder; Derrick Dunn, and Reginald Capers.

My nieces and nephews: Lynn, Mahki, Kyle, Derrick, Johnathan, Adrian, Tonka, April, Jeffrey, Nicholas, Joffrey, Lashaunn, Greg, Demetrius, Indy, Jeremy, and Allison.

My cousins: Especially Herman, Martha, Ocie, Mary, Paula, Homer D., Paula, Brandi, Briann, Ralph, Glorie, Issa, Kenneth, Lola, Earl, Louis, Andy, Nancy, Dwylan, Charlene, Meco, Lamar, Dwylan Meco, Jr; Lola Hanks Spann; James, Chastity, Robin, Dantavious, Felicia, Willie Joe, Willie Joe, Jr, Erica, and Jermaine

My extended Family (Blood) -- Eunice Williams Gordon, my mother-in-law; Shirley and Leon Powell; Sam and Barbara McCray; Gayle and William McGregor; Delphenia and Curtis Rollins; Romona and Waikila Johnson: Fred Johnson and Family; Wanda and Checree McCray; Randall, Sheila, Ebony, and Kenya McCray: Sylvia, Ron, Shameeka, and Jelani Gamble, Jo and Johnathan Barbot; Betty Williams; Joseph Gordon; Marion Gordon; Johnnie, Clara, and Brian Armstrong; John , Dawn, John Jr., Chelsea, and Christopher Whittaker; and Marion and Carlise Gordon.

My extended Family (Friendship and Spirit): The Pappy's: Ethel and Roz;
The McMillian's: Jimmy, Glenda, Beverly, Janice, and Buck;
the Ford-Thompson's: Michael, Chalmer, Noni, Midiwa, and Gyasi; The Chamberlain's: Lafayette, Martha, Athena, Kim, and Cassietta; The Greer's: Charles, Rosalyn, and Joshua; The Reeder's (Redell, Brenda, Gayla, Charity, and Jessie); The Morris's: Carl, Debbie, Henry, and William; The Streeter's: Willie, Dee, Latrease, and Lebaron; the Stovall's: Louis, Estella, Marvin, Victor and Daisy; The Hill's: Walter, Jill, Shaka, Askia, and Ose'; The Morton's (Bob, Mary Lou, Brandy, and Deven); The McDonald's, posthumously,: Lorenius and Salina; The Wheelers: Ed, Sue, Wendi, Dawn, Loren, and Kiana; the Gordon's: Thurman, Maya, and Maura; the Assensoh's: A.B., Yvette, Kwadoo, and Livingston; the Hunter's : Homer, Lucille, Cathy, Jerrilyn, Brenda, and Reginald; the Hunter's: Oliver, Eve, and Page; The Vance's: William, Debra, and Robert.

Extra Special Friends: Reginald Willingham; Michael Stalling; Doreleena Sammons Posey; Livia Sapp Hardin; Robin Harleston; Manley Elliot Banks; The Tubbs, Juanita and Leanne; The Isoms:Vincent, Clarisa, and Averi, my god-daughter; Herbie Leveatt; Freddie Mae Wiggins: Pauline Warrick; Annie Dunn; Dina Dunn: Mae Willie Jackson; Juanita Hawkins; Irene Thornton; Roselle S. English; Noni Taylor, Mary Marble; Rocelle and Rose Prise; The Roderick Van Royals; James Mumford; Mignonne Snipes; Anthony Robinson; James Daniels; Floyd Hodge; Harvey and Nedra Smith; and Claude and Carolyn Glover.

The Men of Kappa Alpha Psi, especially Pi Chapter, and my sands of The Riot Squad '73: Byron Brooks, John Dameron, Walter Dogan, Harold D. Trulear, Willie Woodruff, and Rod Smith. Special kudos to Brother Roosevelt Galloway for preserving the history of Pi Chapter.

The Men of Morehouse College
The Women of Spelman College
The Students of Tuskegee University
The Students of Livingstone College
The Citizens of Fort Gaines and Clay County Georgia

My church homes of my spiritual journey: The Saint Luke Missionary Baptist Church (Clay County Georgia); the Springfield Baptist Church, Fort Gaines, Georgia; The Hillside Truth Center, Atlanta, Georgia; and the Second Baptist Church, Bloomington, IN

The Hanks-Turner Heritage Association, especially the Albert Hanks'; the John Turner's; the Lougenia Glenn's; the Peter Hanks'; the Roxie Brown's; the Trudie Chester's; the Laura Hanks', and the Tom Hanks'.

The family members of the Turner-McSwain Family Reunion
The family members of the Mays-Powell Family Reunion

My research assistants, Elgin Rogers, Jas Sullivan, Richard Burden, Doris Clark and Dennis Laffoon, of Laffoon Design & Marketing for page and cover design.

Preface

The Alphabet of Self-Esteem: An Inspirational Journal for Successful Living

So much of what ails individuals in western society is rooted in the false belief that they lack value. Human beings develop all manner of maladies because some judgments outside of themselves have deemed them less than optimal. These outside human societal constructions include gender, race, sexual orientation, degree of melanin, religion, national origin, region, accent, weight, physical size, and proportionality, and the list goes on ad infinitum, i.e., endlessly.

The key to overcoming any of these maladies is to know "who" and "whose" you are. You are a child of the timeless intelligence that brings order to the cosmos. As a part of the same divinity that causes the cosmos to synchronize in perfect harmony, you are essentially and fundamentally perfect just as you are. God does not make mistakes and everything that you are is a part of the creator's plan for you and his universe. Our job is to know that we are royalty because we are children of the King of Kings.

The Alphabet of Self-Esteem: An Inspirational Journal for Successful Living is a personal empowerment tool. It speaks to the inherent worth of every human being. The human potential is unlimited—the goal of this journal is to provide words of inspiration as well as a place to write down your dreams, goals, and desires. Moreover, this journal is a place to develop an action plan for you to become all that you can be—a fully optimized human being whose energy is focused on moving our world culture towards greater levels of divinity. As fully optimized human being, we can help to foster a world that will be in alignment with God's plan for the heavens, the earth, and all of his creation.

Lawrence J. Hanks
June 14, 2003
Bloomington, IN

Preface: Part II

Life often gets in the way of living.
Life is the combination of all the things that we do in order to be responsible persons: we bathe, we brush our teeth, we use deodorant, we make sure our children bath, brush their teeth, and use deodorant. We get where we need to be, with what we need to have, while attempting to either do it for our children or making sure that they are doing it themselves. I will not mention making sure that the bills are paid and the house is clean and remembering to be all the things that you are supposed to be: spouse, child, friend, sibling, bread winner, responsible citizen, etc.

Living is finding those rare moments when you get to focus on your dreams. Whatever the dreams are, living is when you have the time to push them closer to reality. Maybe your dream is writing a book, a play, a thesis, a dissertation, or a series of letters to your children or grandchildren who are not yet born. Maybe your dream is getting closer to God, researching your family tree, or getting that elusive college degree, MBA, LLD, or Ph.D. Perhaps you want to draw, paint, raise children, tell stories,.... You get the message. You are the only who truly knows what your heart and spirit longs to be or do.

My vision for *The Alphabet of Self- Esteem: An Inspirational Journal for Successful Living* is that it will be a vehicle to get you from "life" to "living." My prayer is that it will inspire you to write down your thoughts and dreams. Writing them down is the first step toward bringing them from the world of ideas into the material world.

Name it (your dream) and claim it.

Write down the vision and make it plain.

Plan your work and work your plan

Believe it, develop your plan, and achieve it

Get past life and get to living

Lawrence J. Hanks
July 12, 2003
Fort Gaines, GA

A **is for ANSWER:** The answers to all my challenges are within me. No other entity can defy the power of the good that is within. With a positive mental attitude and positive action, I create actualization.

B **is for BETTER:** Everyday in every way, I am getting better and better and better.

C **is for CAN:** I can achieve whatever I am capable of conceiving and believing.

D **is for DETERMINATION:** I will not allow anyone to deter me from my goals. I will keep my eyes on the prize.

E **is for EXCELLENT:** The only acceptable standard for someone of my brilliance and capabilities.

F **is for FEARLESS:** There is nothing to fear but fear itself. In all places, in all times, under all conditions, I am divinely protected.

G **is for GIFTED:** I am the manifestation of ancient wisdom. My brain is the most complex computer ever designed.

H **is for HIGHER:** Higher and higher I go, mentally, physically, and spiritually. Where I'll stop, nobody knows.

I **is for INGENIOUS:** I am capable of clever combinations and complex contrivance.

J **is for JUDICIOUS:** I am capable of discrete and sound judgment. I am not always right, but I'm seldom wrong.

K **is for KNOWLEDGEABLE:** I am demonstrative with my intelligence. I apprehend truth; my fine gray matter is finely tuned– I am cognizant of my powers of cognition.

L **is for LAVISH:** I am capable of producing profusely. My potential is ample and abundant. I am capable of exceeding the average. I have more than the usual power, capacity, and scope.

M **is for MAJOR:** For I am certainly not minor. I am superior in rank, status, and performance. I am as BAD as I choose to be.

N **is for NATTY:** I am trimly neat, clean, smart, and tidy.

O **is for OMNIFICENT:** I am "unlimited in creative power" I optimize my opulent potential.

P **is for PAR:** As in par excellence – I strive for excellence in the highest degree, pre-eminently so. I peak at my pinnacles when I am perfect. The positive permeates my persona. Perseverance pervades my personality.

Q **is for QUALITY:** I have the skills, training, and ability for many special purposes. I question all that I do not understand. I quiver at my own quick wittedness.

R **is for RECTITUDE:** I strive to be morally correct. I strive to be relevant and reliable. I reason and ruminate over my actions. Thus, the ramifications will not be random. With the radix of my quest being deeply rooted in the universal order, I can rambunctiously raise my rank.

S **is for SELF-ACTUALIZATION:** I will strive to be the best that I can be. I will sacrifice and sanitize the sacred sanctum of my mind. I am suave, shrewd, sagacious, sentimental and serene. I will strive to satiate my savant ambitions. I will succeed.

T **is for TENACIOUS:** I cannot be pulled apart. Through thick and thin I have toiled, tirelessly towards the top. I am thankful for my terseness, tactfulness, and thaumathurgic nature. I am torrid in my attempt to be triumphant. My quest for excellence is a tour de force.

U **is for UTMOST:** I will utilize my unlimited potential until I have reached the ultimate. Given the ubiquitous nature of opportunities for success, I will unrelentingly upgrade skills; I will pursue my goals with unflagging zeal, unfeigned affection, unmitigated gall, unconditional love, and unadulterated enthusiasm.

V **is for VERACITY:** The truth will set me free– truth crushed to the earth will rise again. Venerate virtue for it is not vapid; it is valid, vital, victorious, vast, viable, versatile, vivacious, valuable, and voluminous. I will develop the verve and the vision to vanquish vice for it is vincible.

W **is for WISDOM:** I am well, wise, whole, wealthy, and wonderful. My life is workable for I have been weaned of all weakness and wickedness.

X **is for XEROPHILOUS:** I am capable of not only surviving but prospering in environments that are deficient in the ingredients that facilitate life. I push on despite the apparent adversities of life.

Y **is for YEARN:** I persistently desire to keep on keeping on. I will not yield to mediocrity.

Z **is for ZEAL:** I have unlimited energy and focus to execute all of my plans. I will remain persistent and patient as I aggressively pursue my goals.

A B C D E F G H I J K L M N O P Q R S T U V W X Y Z

A

is for
Answer

The answer to all my challenges are within me. No other entity can defy the power of the good that is within. With a positive mental attitude and positive action, I create actualization.

A
B
C
D
E
F
G
H
I
J
K
L
M
N
O
P
Q
R
S
T
U
V
W
X
Y
Z

B

B is for Better

Everyday in every way,
I am getting better
and better and better.

A
B
C
D
E
F
G
H
I
J
K
L
M
N
O
P
Q
R
S
T
U
V
W
X
Y
Z

A
B
C
D
E
F
G
H
I
J
K
L
M
N
O
P
Q
R
S
T
U
V
W
X
Y
Z

B

C

C is for
Can

I can achieve whatever
I am capable of
conceiving and believing.

C

A
B
C
D
E
F
G
H
I
J
K
L
M
N
O
P
Q
R
S
T
U
V
W
X
Y
Z

A
B
C
D
E
F
G
H
I
J
K
L
M
N
O
P
Q
R
S
T
U
V
W
X
Y
Z

A B **C** D E F G H I J K L M N O P Q R S T U V W X Y Z

D

D is for
Determination

I will not allow anyone to
deter me from my goals.
I will keep my eyes on the prize.

A
B
C
D
E
F
G
H
I
J
K
L
M
N
O
P
Q
R
S
T
U
V
W
X
Y
Z

E

E is for
Excellent

A B C D E F G H I J K L M N O P Q R S T U V W X Y Z

Excellence is the only acceptable standard for someone of my brilliance and capabilities.

A B C D **E** F G H I J K L M N O P Q R S T U V W X Y Z

F

F is for Fearless

There is nothing to
fear but fear itself.
In all places, in all times,
under all conditions,
I am divinely protected.

A B C D E **F** G H I J K L M N O P Q R S T U V W X Y Z

G

G is for
Gifted

A B C D E F G H I J K L M N O P Q R S T U V W X Y Z

I am the manifestation of ancient wisdom.
My brain is the most complex
computer ever designed.

H

 is for
Higher

Higher and higher I go, mentally,
physically, and spiritually.
Where I'll stop, nobody knows.

A B C D E F G **H** I J K L M N O P Q R S T U V W X Y Z

H

A
B
C
D
E
F
G
H
I
J
K
L
M
N
O
P
Q
R
S
T
U
V
W
X
Y
Z

I

I is for
Ingenious

ABCDEFGH**I**JKLMNOPQRSTUVWXYZ

I am capable of clever combinations
and complex contrivance.

A
B
C
D
E
F
G
H
I
J
K
L
M
N
O
P
Q
R
S
T
U
V
W
X
Y
Z

A
B
C
D
E
F
G
H
I
J
K
L
M
N
O
P
Q
R
S
T
U
V
W
X
Y
Z

J

 is for
Judicious

J

I am capable of discrete
and sound judgment.
I am not always right,
but I'm seldom wrong.

A
B
C
D
E
F
G
H
I
J
K
L
M
N
O
P
Q
R
S
T
U
V
W
X
Y
Z

A B C D E F G H I J K L M N O P Q R S T U V W X Y Z

A B C D E F G H I J K L M N O P Q R S T U V W X Y Z

K

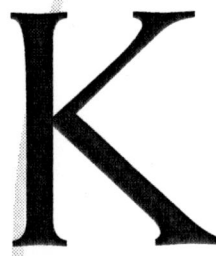 is for
Knowledgeable

A
B
C
D
E
F
G
H
I
J
K
L
M
N
O
P
Q
R
S
T
U
V
W
X
Y
Z

I am demonstrative with my
intelligence. I apprehend truth;
my fine gray matter is finely tuned–
I am cognizant of my powers of cognition.

A B C D E F G H I J **K** L M N O P Q R S T U V W X Y Z

L

L is for
Lavish

I am capable of producing profusely.
My potential is ample and abundant.
I am capable of exceeding the average.
I have more than the usual power,
capacity, and scope.

L

A B C D E F G H I J K L M N O P Q R S T U V W X Y Z

L

A B C D E F G H I J K L M N O P Q R S T U V W X Y Z

M

M is for
Major

A B C D E F G H I J K L **M** N O P Q R S T U V W X Y Z

For I am certainly not minor.
I am superior in rank, status, and performance.
I am as BAD as I choose to be.

A
B
C
D
E
F
G
H
I
J
K
L
M
N
O
P
Q
R
S
T
U
V
W
X
Y
Z

A
B
C
D
E
F
G
H
I
J
K
L
M
N
O
P
Q
R
S
T
U
V
W
X
Y
Z

N

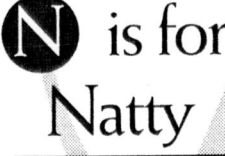 is for
Natty

I am trimly neat,
clean, smart, and tidy.

A
B
C
D
E
F
G
H
I
J
K
L
M
N
O
P
Q
R
S
T
U
V
W
X
Y
Z

A
B
C
D
E
F
G
H
I
J
K
L
M
N
O
P
Q
R
S
T
U
V
W
X
Y
Z

A
B
C
D
E
F
G
H
I
J
K
L
M
N
O
P
Q
R
S
T
U
V
W
X
Y
Z

O

O is for Omnificent

I am unlimited in creative power
I optimize my opulent potential.

A B C D E F G H I J K L M N O P Q R S T U V W X Y Z

A B C D E F G H I J K L M N **O** P Q R S T U V W X Y Z

P

P is for Par

As in par excellence –
I strive for excellence to the
highest degree, pre-eminently so.
I peak at my pinnacles when I am perfect.
The positive permeates my persona.
Perseverance pervades my personality.

A B C D E F G H I J K L M N O P Q R S T U V W X Y Z

A
B
C
D
E
F
G
H
I
J
K
L
M
N
O
P
Q
R
S
T
U
V
W
X
Y
Z

P

Q is for Quality

I have the skills, training,
and ability for many special purposes.
I question all that I do not understand.
I quiver at my own quick wittedness.

A B C D E F G H I J K L M N O P Q R S T U V W X Y Z

A
B
C
D
E
F
G
H
I
J
K
L
M
N
O
P
Q
R
S
T
U
V
W
X
Y
Z

A B C D E F G H I J K L M N O P Q R S T U V W X Y Z

R

R is for
Rectitude

I strive to be morally correct.
I strive to be relevant and reliable.
I reason and ruminate over my actions.
Thus, the ramifications will not be random.
With the radix of my quest being
deeply rooted in the universal order,
I can rambunctiously raise my rank.

A
B
C
D
E
F
G
H
I
J
K
L
M
N
O
P
Q
R
S
T
U
V
W
X
Y
Z

A B C D E F G H I J K L M N O P Q R S T U V W X Y Z

S

S is for
Self-Actualization

I will strive to be
the best that I can be.
I will sacrifice and sanitize
the sacred sanctum of my mind.
I am suave, shrewd, sagacious,
sentimental and serene.
I will strive to satiate
my savant ambitions.
I will succeed.

A
B
C
D
E
F
G
H
I
J
K
L
M
N
O
P
Q
R
S
T
U
V
W
X
Y
Z

A
B
C
D
E
F
G
H
I
J
K
L
M
N
O
P
Q
R
S
T
U
V
W
X
Y
Z

T

T is for
Tenacious

A
B
C
D
E
F
G
H
I
J
K
L
M
N
O
P
Q
R
S
T
U
V
W
X
Y
Z

I cannot be pulled apart.
Through thick and thin I have toiled,
tirelessly towards the top.
I am thankful for my terseness,
tactfulness, and thaumathurgic nature.
I am torrid in my attempt to be triumphant.
My quest for excellence is a tour de force.

A B C D E F G H I J K L M N O P Q R S T U V W X Y Z

A B C D E F G H I J K L M N O P Q R S T **u** V W X Y Z

U

U is for
Utmost

I will utilize my unlimited potential
until I have reached the ultimate.
Given the ubiquitous nature of
opportunities for success,
I will unrelentingly upgrade skills:
I will pursue my goals with unflagging zeal,
unfeigned affection, unmitigated gall,
unconditional love,
and unadulterated enthusiasm.

A B C D E F G H I J K L M N O P Q R S T U V W X Y Z

A B C D E F G H I J K L M N O P Q R S T U V W X Y Z

A B C D E F G H I J K L M N O P Q R S T U V W X Y Z

U

V

V is for
Veracity

The truth will set you free,
truth crushed to the earth will rise again.
Venerate virtue for it is not vapid;
it is valid, vital, victorious, vast, viable,
versatile, vivacious, valuable, and voluminous.
I will develop the vigor and the vision
to vanquish vice for it is vincible.

A
B
C
D
E
F
G
H
I
J
K
L
M
N
O
P
Q
R
S
T
U
V
W
X
Y
Z

A
B
C
D
E
F
G
H
I
J
K
L
M
N
O
P
Q
R
S
T
U
V
W
X
Y
Z

W

 is for
Wisdom

I am well, wise, whole,
wealthy, and wonderful.
My life is workable
for I have been weaned of
all weakness and wickedness.

A B C D E F G H I J K L M N O P Q R S T U V **W** X Y Z

A B C D E F G H I J K L M N O P Q R S T U V **W** X Y Z

X

 is for
Xerophilous

I am capable of not only surviving but prospering in environments that are deficient in the ingredients that facilitate life.
I push on despite the apparent adversities of life.

A
B
C
D
E
F
G
H
I
J
K
L
M
N
O
P
Q
R
S
T
U
V
W
X
Y
Z

A B C D E F G H I J K L M N O P Q R S T U V W X Y Z

Y

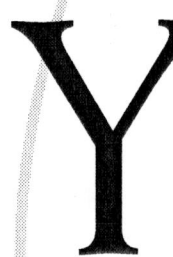

 is for Yearn

I persistently desire to
keep on keeping on.
I will not yield to mediocrity.

A
B
C
D
E
F
G
H
I
J
K
L
M
N
O
P
Q
R
S
T
U
V
W
X
Y
Z

A
B
C
D
E
F
G
H
I
J
K
L
M
N
O
P
Q
R
S
T
U
V
W
X
Y
Z

Z

Z is for
Zeal

I have unlimited energy and
focus to execute all of my plans.
I will remain persistent and patient as
I aggressively pursue my goals.

A B C D E F G H I J K L M N O P Q R S T U V W X Y Z

A
B
C
D
E
F
G
H
I
J
K
L
M
N
O
P
Q
R
S
T
U
V
W
X
Y
Z

About the Author

Lawrence J. Hanks is an Associate Professor of Political Science at Indiana University-Bloomington. He is a **magna cum laude** graduate of Morehouse College and earned a Ph.D. in Government from Harvard University. He is the husband of Diane Gordon Hanks and the father of four children: Shonda Latrice, L. Julius, II, Latoysha Joy, and Mahogany Arlette. Dr. Hanks has been a passionate teacher, solutionist, and advocate of positive thought for over twenty-five years. *The Alphabet of Self-Esteem: An Inspirational Journal for Successful Living* is his fifth book.

Dr. Hanks is available for consulting, workshops, and speaking engagements. He may be reached at (812) 855-9752. His e-mail address is lhanks@indiana.edu.

Printed in the United States
17234LVS00003B/337-384